OLYSLAGER AUTO LIBRARY

American Trucks of the Early Thirties

compiled by the OLYSLAGER ORGANISATION
edited by Bart H. Vanderveen

FREDERICK WARNE & Co Ltd
London and New York

THE OLYSLAGER AUTO LIBRARY

This book is one of a growing range of titles on major transport subjects.
Titles published so far include:

The Jeep
Half-Tracks
Scammell Vehicles
Fire-Fighting Vehicles 1840–1950
Earthmoving Vehicles
Wreckers and Recovery Vehicles
Passenger Vehicles 1893–1940
Buses and Coaches from 1940
Fairground and Circus Transport

American Cars of the 1930s
American Cars of the 1940s
American Cars of the 1950s
American Trucks of the Early Thirties

British Cars of the Early Thirties
British Cars of the Late Thirties
British Cars of the Early Forties
British Cars of the Late Forties

Copyright © Olyslager Organisation BV 1974

Library of Congress Catalog Card No. 74-80616

ISBN 0 7232 1803 X

Filmset and printed in Great Britain
by BAS Printers Limited, Wallop, Hampshire
799.574

This book is intended to represent a cross-section of trucks of various types of American manufacture or origin. To cover five years of production fully in one book, large or small, is an impossible task and therefore a random selection has been made, with the emphasis on the better-known makes.

Coverage is by no means restricted to trucks built, bodied and operated in North America, if only because this would not give a fair picture of the situation. Hundreds of thousands of American trucks were exported for service in all corners of the world. Most of these 'foreigners' were exported in CKD (completely knocked down) form and assembled in the country of destination. In the process certain modifications could be made, varying from installing non-standard components in an otherwise 'standard' US type to importing only certain major components or assemblies, and manufacturing the other parts. In practically all cases the bodywork was built locally and in many instances the cab as well. What was usually needed in export markets was the running chassis with the front end sheet metal, in as small a pack as possible. American chassis were extremely good value for money, fast, reliable and built to last. They sold competitively almost everywhere, even in West European countries such as Britain and France, which had their own motor industry. In addition to trucks used for carrying general cargo, the book shows special-purpose derivatives; in fact, many of the trucks at this time were bodied if not built to suit the particular requirements of the customers. Also included are some buses, based on special long-wheelbase truck chassis variants, rather than purpose built.

In the United States the truck was responsible for a drastic change in the economy and in the general way of life. By the end of the 1930s some 54,000 communities had no railroads and depended solely on motor vehicles. These communities had been virtually 'created' by the motor truck. Over 30% of all trucks were in rural areas where they had become the foundation of a better standard of living.

In 1930 there were more than 80 truck manufacturers in the USA. Some were small specialist firms, willing and able to assemble almost any kind of truck their customer required, installing engines, transmissions, axles, brakes, etc. bought from other specialist firms which concentrated on the production of those components. Such truck builders, together with the medium-sized ones, offered a wide range of models to select from.

The large-volume producers, on the other hand (Ford, General Motors, Chrysler) produced considerable quantities of a few basic models, often using variants of the engines of their contemporary passenger cars. This, too, changed gradually when the 'Big Three' expanded their ranges. By the end of the decade many of the original makes had disappeared, having merged with others, been liquidated, or finished for other reasons. The remaining firms had become better established although many of those have now also ceased to exist, again usually after take-overs by, or mergers with, the strongest.

Unlike passenger cars and the commercial vehicles of the 'Big Three', American trucks were not face-lifted in an almost annual cycle. The heaviest models in particular did not change much at all, making it difficult to date them accurately.

Additional pictures and details of American trucks, panel vans, buses, etc. of this era are included in our books *American Cars of the 1930s, Wreckers and Recovery Vehicles, Half-Tracks, Passenger Vehicles* and *The Observer's Fighting Vehicles Directory*.

Piet Olyslager MSIA, MSAE, KIVI

INTRODUCTION

1930 In 1930 the total number of trucks and buses in the world was 5¾ million. Of this total, 3,715,100 units or 64·4% were in the United States. Most of these were trucks, namely 3,674,593 (40 years later this number had grown to 17½ million!). During the year 575,364 new trucks and buses were sold from US plants, valued at nearly $4 million. Best-sellers were Ford (197,216 new registrations) and Chevrolet (118,253), followed by International (23,703) and Dodge Brothers (15,558), all others being under 10,000 each. Owing to the Depression, however, sales of both cars and trucks declined throughout the year and it was not until 1934 that sales took an upward swing again. In contrast to the above figures, the British motor industry during 1930 produced 66,859 commercial vehicles and buses, and the total number of such vehicles on British roads in September was 102,791—less than the annual truck production of Ford or Chevrolet, and less than a quarter of the total number of trucks which in the US found their way to the scrap-heaps!

1931 United States motor truck and bus factory sales in 1931 totalled 432,262. On the road now were slightly fewer than in 1930, namely 3,655,835 trucks and about 42,000 buses. Ford, Chevrolet, International and Dodge were truck sales leaders again, with 138,854, 99,600, 21,073 and 13,518 units respectively.

Other well-known truck manufacturers were Autocar, Brockway, Diamond T, Federal, FWD, GMC, Indiana, Mack, Oshkosh, Reo, Sterling, Stewart, Studebaker, Ward LaFrance, White and Willys. Lesser known names and smaller firms included Acme, American LaFrance, Armleder, Atterbury, Biederman, Chicago, Clinton, Clydesdale, Condor, Corbitt, Day-Elder, Denby, Duplex, Eagle, Fageol, Fisher-Standard, Garford, Gramm, Kissel, Larrabee, Maccar, Marmon-Herrington, Moreland, Pierce-Arrow, Relay, Republic, Rugby, Sanford, Schacht and Selden. Many of these fitted bought-in major components and assemblies such as engines from Buda, Continental, Hall Scott (ACF), Hercules, Lycoming, Waukesha and Wisconsin, transmissions from Brown-Lipe, Clark, Fuller, Warner and others, axles from Clark, Eaton, Timken, steering gears from Gemmer, Saginaw, Ross, etc.

1932 Motor truck and bus factory sales this year numbered only 228,303, less than half the 1930 figure. This was, of course, caused by the gloomy economic climate of the deepening Depression.

Passenger car production was also well down, from almost 2·8 million in 1930 to 1·1 million. The total number of trucks in use in the US was just under 3½ million, still a great deal more than in all the world's other nations together. New truck registrations for 1932 by make showed Ford still in the lead with 66,937, but now closely followed by Chevrolet with 60,784 (General Motors' Chevrolet and GMC combined outsold Ford by just over 200!). International Harvester Co. was still firmly in third place, with 15,752 new registrations, followed by Chrysler's Dodge with only 8744 (but destined to do better than International in the following year).

1933 Truck and bus sales were on the upswing, with 329,218 units sold by US plants. Total vehicle registrations were slightly down, but trucks and buses were up. New truck registrations by make put Chevrolet in first place with 99,880, followed by Ford with 62,397, Dodge with 28,034 and International with 26,658. Chevrolet kept their lead over Ford until 1969, with the exceptions of 1935 and 1937. White, who sold 1384 trucks this year, developed a new type of bus, a coach in fact, with underfloor horizontally-opposed 12-cylinder 'pancake' engine. It was fitted to a new range of trucks in 1934. Diesel engines also began to make their appearance in US-made trucks although their installation was usually by the operators themselves, rather than as original equipment; this came later, after the manufacturers had had time and opportunity to carry out experimental developments to a point where they could take full responsibility for the design and operation of such vehicles and be sure of their reliability.

1934 New truck registrations in the United States in 1934 totalled 403,886 and were led by Chevrolet with 157,507, followed by Ford with 128,250. Dodge was third with 48,252, International fourth with 31,555 and GMC fifth with 10,449. Other makes were all under 6,000. Actual factory sales of trucks and buses were 576,205; this probably included exports. For the first time production was higher than in 1930 and this trend was going to continue until 1938. Total vehicle registrations were more than 25¼ million, which included 21½ million passenger cars. It was estimated that all these vehicles together during this year travelled a total distance of 216 billion miles!

5A Autocar

5A: **Autocar** Model SD Six-cylinder Dispatch truck was a 2-ton model with 150- or 174-in wheelbase and 32 × 6 tyres. It was also available with single rear tyres as 1½-ton Model SA. Both had a 60-bhp Autocar L-head Six engine with four-speed gearbox. They were the smallest of the maker's 1930 model range.

5B: **Autocar** of Ardmore, Pennsylvania, were among the few heavy-duty truck builders who were not just assemblers of bought-in engines and other components. Although this could mean lower production costs, these manufacturers had to invest capital in design, development and production tooling themselves. This platform truck of about 1932, but photographed much later, featured a simple open-fronted cab with roll-down side curtains.

5C: **Autocar** Model N 4-ton chassis/cab with coke delivery body. This truck had a 94-bhp Autocar SCH six-cylinder engine of 404 CID and also a transmission and rear axle of own manufacture. It had 9·75-20 tyres and vacuum-assisted hydraulic brakes.

5B Autocar

5C Autocar

7A Brockway

7B Brockway

7B: **Brockway** truck of 1930, in service with the Department of Water Supply, Gas and Electricity of the City of New York. Brockways at this time were similar to Indiana trucks (*q.v.*), the latter company being part of Brockway Trucks, Inc. during 1928–32. The Indiana factory in Marion, Indiana, was the headquarters of Brockway's Western Division, the Eastern Division being at the main plant in Cortland, New York. In 1932 the Marion plant was acquired by White.

7C Brockway

7A: **Brockway** Model 140C, delivered to a Syracuse, NY, brewery in 1933. This model had a six-cylinder Continental Model 30B engine, Brown-Lipe four-speed transmission and Wisconsin double-reduction full-floating rear axle.

7C: **Brockway** in 1934 offered 'America's largest capacity truck', their Model V-1200. Powered by a 753 CID American LaFrance V-12-cylinder engine of 240 bhp, it could haul loads of up to 60,000 lb at sustained speeds of 45 mph.

8A Chevrolet

8A : **Chevrolet** LR Series Universal was identical in appearance to the LQ of 1929. It was a 1½-tonner with 131-in wheelbase and 194 CID overhead-valve Six engine (the famous 'Cast Iron Wonder' or 'Stovebolt Six'). This is a surviving pickup truck, photographed in Stamford, Connecticut, in 1967.

8B : **Chevrolet** trucks were made to last, as witnessed by this 1930 customized right-hand drive job still operating in Malta a few years ago.

8C : Another early **Chevrolet** Six 1½-ton truck, also after having undergone several modifications. This specimen was seen still at work in a Paris suburb in 1966.

8D : **Chevrolet** 1931 Model AE car-derived commercial chassis with ice-cream van body, beautifully restored and preserved in the Mahy collection in Belgium. Built in Great Britain.

8C Chevrolet

8B Chevrolet

8D Chevrolet

9A: **Chevrolet** trucks for 1931 (named Independence) differed from the preceding 1930 models in having the same front end styling as the 1931 model Chevrolet car, albeit with painted radiator shell and headlamps. Headlamp tie bar and front wings were the same as on 1929/30 models. 131- and 157-in wheelbase chassis were available, with either single or dual rear tyres. Shown is a Model LT with Dutch cab and hand-operated tipper body.

9B: **Chevrolet** Series M, introduced during 1931, had several mechanical improvements. One is shown here with factory-supplied stake body.

9C: **Chevrolet** Series LT, built in Great Britain in 1931 and direct ancestor of the Bedford Truck. This beautifully preserved 30-cwt truck with dropside body belongs to Mr Ken Taylor of St Helier, Jersey, CI.

9A Chevrolet

9B Chevrolet

9C Chevrolet

CHEVROLET

10A Chevrolet

10C Chevrolet

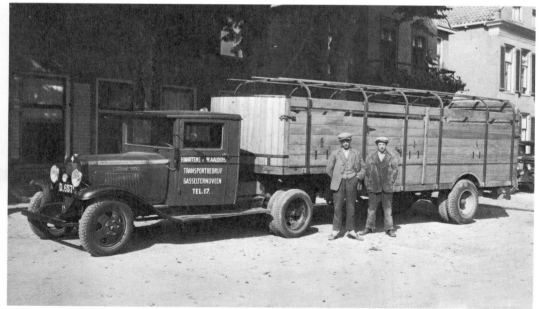

10B Chevrolet

10A: **Chevrolet** Confederate Series BA Sedan Delivery of late 1932 was basically similar to the contemporary Series BA car. It had 18-in wire wheels and 109-in wheelbase.

10B: **Chevrolet** 1932 Confederate Series NB 1½-ton tractor truck with semi-trailer in the Netherlands. 1932 Chevrolet trucks were available with two wheelbase sizes, 131-in (shown) and 157-in, and with single or dual rear tyres.

10C: **Chevrolet** ND 157-in wheelbase platform truck of 1932. In appearance the 1932 truck models were very similar to those of 1931. The engine was a 194 CID OHV Six.

11A Chevrolet

11A: **Chevrolet** 1933 CB Master ½-ton commercial chassis with door-to-door delivery van body. 1933 Chevrolet trucks had the same front end styling as the 1932 passenger cars except for the bonnet (hood) which had louvres instead of doors.

11B: **Chevrolet** Series OA 1½-ton truck as supplied in 1933 to the Field Artillery of the US Army. Military requirements included fitting of radiator and headlight brush guard, tow hooks, etc. Note spare wheel mounting.

11C: **Chevrolet** broke away from its customary use of passenger car front end sheet metal for their trucks. Although reminiscent of the 1933 car, the 1934 truck front end was specially made. Shown is a ½-ton Model DB with 109-in wheelbase. The OHV Six engine now had 206 cu. in displacement and developed 60 bhp at 3000 rpm.

11B Chevrolet

11C Chevrolet

CHICAGO TRUCKS

Prompt information will be sent distributors and prospective representatives throughout the world, concerning the highly profitable opportunity afforded by a complete Export Line of heavy duty chassis trucks.

All Chicago Trucks are of Heavy Duty Chassis construction—beautiful in line—but built for rugged, long-lived, dependable service combined with all the speed required by users.

MODELS

Bevel Drive	Standard Wheelbases (others optional)
2 ton 6 cylinder	140", 152", 164", 176"
2½ ton 6 cylinder	154-5/16", 166-5/16", 178-5/16", 190-5/16"
Worm Drive	
3 ton 6 cylinder	154-5/16", 166-5/16", 178-5/16", 190-5/16"
4 ton 6 cylinder	154-5/16", 166-5/16", 178-5/16", 190-5/16"
5 ton 6 cylinder	146", 158", 170", 182"
Worm Drive Six-Wheelers	
8 ton 6 cylinder	186½", 198½", 210"
10-12 ton 6 cylinder	186½", 198½", 210"

All parts used in the manufacture of

CHICAGO TRUCKS

are standard products of well known manufacturers, such as:

Timken Axles,
Waukesha Engines,
Brown-Lipe Transmission,
Zenith Carburetors,
Auto Lite System,
Four-Wheel Lockheed Hydraulic Brakes,
etc.

Steadily increasing sales of Chicago Trucks in all countries prove—in themselves—the highest testimonials of quickly recognized and appreciated values, quality and dependability.

Increased productive capacity and greatly extended executive facilities, made possible by enlargement of our factory, enable us to offer and deliver the promptest and most satisfactory service to our overseas clients.

Chicago Trucks are built in 2 Ton up to 12 Ton capacities—including six wheelers.

You may write if you choose. But our code word "INFORMATION" and your signature cabled to us will bring full and promptest particulars.

CHICAGO MOTOR TRUCKS

401 North Ogden Ave., Chicago, Ill., U. S. A.

Cable Address: "CHITRUCK" All Codes.

12A Chicago

12B Condor

12C Corbitt

12A: **Chicago** trucks were assembled from bought-in components during 1919-32. A wide range of models, from 2- to 12-ton capacity, was listed in this advertisement of November 1930.
12B: **Condor** Model CB 1½–2-ton truck as produced during 1932-34. Condors were built in Chicago and were strictly export versions of the Gramm truck. This tipper-bodied example operated in the Netherlands and had locally-made bodywork.
12C: **Corbitt** Model 168-FD8 2½-ton 6 × 6 (six-wheeled, six-wheel drive) truck, a special job for the US Army in 1933. This sturdy-looking vehicle was powered by a 113-bhp eight-cylinder Lycoming engine and had a GVW rating of 15,000 lb.

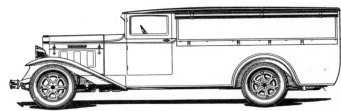

Why DIAMOND·T
MODELS 200 AND 215
are the finest 1-ton trucks built today

Diamond T One-Ton Model 200 (Four-cylinder) and Model 215 (Six-cylinder)

HERE is part of the evidence which proves how much more you get for your money when you invest in a Diamond T. Diamond T trucks are remarkably low priced, because Diamond T's 25 years of experience and strong position in the industry permits such prices. The Diamond T line, from 1 to 12 tons capacity covers every truck need. Write or cable us the words: "DIMON CHICAGO INFORMATION", giving your name and full information will be furnished you at once.

THE ENGINE
of Diamond T Model 200—a truck motor truly of sensational design—develops more than 55 horsepower. Valve areas entirely water jacketed. Full pressure lubrication. Down-draft carburetion. Air cleaner.

CRANKSHAFT DESIGN
Here you see the 3-inch, 5-bearing crankshaft of the Diamond T one-ton Model 200 (four-cylinder) compared with the crankshafts of two other widely sold one-ton trucks.
Here is the secret of the enduring smoothness and freedom from destructive vibration which characterizes Diamond T.
Model 215 (six-cylinder) has a 7-bearing crankshaft of similarly rugged design and accurate balance.

Diamond T

Truck "A"

Truck "B"

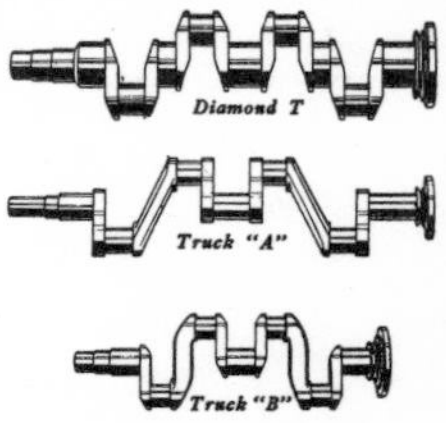

THE DIAMOND-T LINE

Bevel Drive	Wheelbases
1 ton	128½", 135", 158"
1½ ton	138", 156¼", 168"
2 ton	142½", 160¾", 170½", 178¼"
2½ ton	149¾", 158", 168", 178¼", 186¼"

Worm Drive	Wheelbases
2½ ton	142¾", 154", 164", 174", 189", 200"
3 ton	149¾", 159¾", 169¾", 179¾", 189¾", 199¾", 209¾", 221½", 231½"
3½ ton	162", 172", 182", 192", 202", 212", 222"
5 ton	160½", 170½", 180½", 190½", 190½", 200½"

Worm Drive Six-Wheelers	Wheelbases
4 ton	180½", 189½", 199¾", 209¾", 219¾"
6 ton	174½", 180", 190", 200", 210"
8 ton	174¼", 180", 190", 200", 210"
10-12 ton	184", 194", 204", 214", 224"

THE BRAKES
are latest type 4-wheel Hydraulic, internal expanding. Weather-proof. Never require lubrication. Operate identically with truck loaded or empty. Pressure always equalized. Diamond T special molded lining provides high efficiency with minimum wear. Hand brake, contracting type, mounted on propeller shaft.

AXLES ◆ SPRINGS ◆ SHACKLES
The massive full-floating spiral bevel gear axle has a one-piece, heat-treated cast steel housing. Pinion mounted on three rows of ball bearings. Double thrust roller bearings at hubs. Gears and shafts heat-treated alloy steel.
Note extra 4-leaf *helper springs*, which prevent spring breakage. Very rare on any but the costliest trucks.
All spring shackle bushings are *of live rubber*, under constant compression. No greasing, no rattling.

DIAMOND·T MOTOR CAR COMPANY
Export Department
431 South Dearborn Street, Chicago, Illinois, U. S. A.
Cable Address: **DIMON, CHICAGO**   Factories at Chicago

13C Diamond T

13A Day-Elder

13B Diamond T

13A: **Day-Elder** Model 160 3-tonner was one of eleven Super-Service-Sixes announced by the National Motor Manufacturing Co. in 1930. It was an assembled truck, with 81·5-bhp Continental OHV Six engine and Lockheed hydraulic brakes. Day-Elders were made in New Jersey during 1919–37.

13B: **Diamond T** in 1930 more than doubled their export sales. Shown is a dump truck of *c.* 1932 on a road-building project.

13C: **Diamond T** 200 and 215 were 1-ton trucks with 4- and 6-cyl. engines respectively. They were assembled trucks, in this case featuring Buda engine, Borg & Beck clutch, Warner transmission, Timken axles, Ross steering, etc., and renowned for their excellent styling and finish. The makers claimed them to be 'the handsomest trucks in America'.

DIAMOND T

14A Diamond T/Beers

15: **Diamond T/Heil** streamlined road tanker was produced by the Heil Co. of Milwaukee, Wisc., on a Diamond T chassis. The vehicle was 26 feet long and had a capacity of 1500 gallons. The engine was mounted at the rear. The design was originated by Mr H. G. Kizer, Superintendent of Motor Equipment for The Texas Company. The truck was painted in distinctive Texaco red with white raised lettering. 1934

14A: Using **Diamond T** components for the tractor unit, the Dutch importers, NV Adr. Beers of the Hague, produced this semi-trailer bus. Beers also offered similar tractors with diesel engine (e.g. Kromhout-Gardner 4LW).

14B: **Diamond T/Beers** 35-seater Trambus with six-cylinder Hercules engine. Like the semi-trailer bus (14A), it was exhibited at the Amsterdam Motor Show in January 1933.

14C/D: **Diamond T** trucks were entirely restyled in 1934 and featured V-shaped radiator grilles and windscreens and more flowing lines. Hercules engines of various sizes, all with seven-bearing crankshaft, were used throughout the 1½- to 7½-ton range.

14B Diamond T/Beers

14C Diamond T

14D Diamond T

15 Diamond T/Heil

16 : **Dodge Brothers** 3-ton tractor truck with car haulaway semi-trailer, used to transport Chrysler Corporation cars (Chrysler, Dodge, DeSoto, Plymouth) from plants to dealers. Shown is an impressive load of Chryslers in 1930/31. Dodge Brothers trucks were at this time manufactured by Chrysler's Graham Brothers Division.

17A Dodge Brothers

17B Dodge Brothers

17C Dodge Brothers

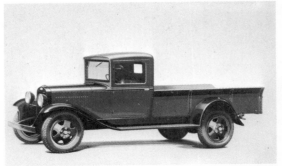

17D Dodge Brothers

17A : **Dodge Brothers** in 1930 offered trucks with payload ratings from $\frac{1}{2}$ to 3 tons, all with their own engines. The $\frac{1}{2}$-ton had a four-cylinder ($3\frac{5}{8} \times 4\frac{1}{4}$ in) engine, the $\frac{3}{4}$-ton had the Four or a Six ($3\frac{3}{8} \times 3\frac{7}{8}$ in). Most were fitted with wooden spoke wheels, as shown on this Express truck (with roll-up side curtains).

17B : **Dodge Brothers** police truck of the early 1930s. It was in service with the police force of Hamtramck, the Detroit suburb where Chrysler's Dodge Brothers car plant was situated.

17C : **Dodge Brothers** trucks were also made in England, at this stage mainly assembled from imported components. This surviving 30-cwt platform truck of 1931 was fully restored in the mid-1960s.

17D : **Dodge Brothers** 1933 trucks were very similar to their 1931/32 predecessors. This is a 1-tonner with factory-supplied cab and pick-up body. During the year a range of completely new models was introduced.

18: **Dodge Brothers** 1½-ton truck was available with four- or six-cylinder engine, model designations being UF30A and F30A respectively. Tyres were 6·00-20 front, 32 × 6 rear. 2- and 3-ton models were also made : these had six-cylinder engines. 1931.

19B Dodge Brothers

19A Dodge

19A: **Dodge** 1933 ½-ton pick-up truck used front end and doors of contemporary Dodge Model DP car. Engine was 75-bhp 201·3 CID L-head Six, wheelbase 115 in. Similar styling was used for 1934 model year's Dodge Brothers trucks (q.v.).

19B: **Dodge Brothers** trucks for 1934 were redesigned and restyled. A typical example of the modernized medium-weight range was this 1½-ton Model K33 with 148-in wheelbase and 78-bhp L-head Six engine. 1935 models were similar. After 1934/5 the marque name of the trucks was changed from Dodge Brothers to Dodge.

19C: **Fargo** trucks were export-only variants of Dodge trucks. They were made available by the Chrysler Corp. for franchise-holders of other-than-Dodge Chrysler makes so that they, too, could sell trucks. This is a 136-in wheelbase 1934 Model KF32, which corresponded with the Dodge K32.

19C Fargo

FEDERAL

20A Federal

20A : **Federal** Model E6 platform truck in Copenhagen, Denmark. The engine was a 60-bhp six-cylinder Continental 17E Red Seal of 215 cu. in capacity, driving through a four-speed Warner gearbox. It had Lockheed hydraulic brakes on all wheels and was produced about 1931.

20B : **Federal** Model DSW 2½ –3-ton was introduced at the end of 1930 and could be ordered with 48-bhp four- or 60-bhp six-cylinder engine and two wheelbase sizes. Of the rear bogie only the front axle was driven. The rear suspension featured twin trunnion-mounted inverted semi-elliptic leaf springs.

20C : In 1934 **Federal** offered a range of light, medium and heavy chassis for truck, bus and tractor applications. Engines were Continental, Hercules and Waukesha four- and six-cylinder units from 50 up to 114 bhp. The rear axle was of the full-floating type.

20B Federal

20C Federal

21A Ford

21C Ford

21A: **Ford** Model A Pickup of 1930 was available with closed cab or soft top as shown. This body style was known as the Roadster Pickup. The Model A and AA trucks were first introduced for the 1928 model year and for 1930 were restyled. They were superseded in production by the Model B and BB for the 1932 model year.

21B: **Ford** Model A Commercial was derived from the Model A car. Both had $103\frac{1}{2}$-in wheelbase and the well-known L-head Four engine. This RHD survivor was assembled and bodied in Britain.

21C: **Ford** Model AA $1\frac{1}{2}$-ton truck was available with $131\frac{1}{2}$- and 157-in wheelbase. The engine was the same as in the Model A ($3\frac{7}{8} \times 4\frac{1}{4}$ in Four), but transmission was four-instead of three-speed. The rear suspension comprised cantilever leaf springs, and either single or dual rear tyres could be specified. In 1930 Ford listed 36 body styles for the Model A and AA chassis. The Model AA chassis price was $520. Shown is an AA-based fire truck in the Netherlands.

21D: **Ford** Model AA $131\frac{1}{2}$-in wb truck as used by the US Army. The illustration shows some of the various special fitments. Note the side-mounted spare wheel and the recess in the cab door.

21B Ford

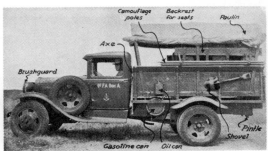

21D Ford

22 : **Ford** Model AA truck as used by the Sudanese Defence Force in the early 1930s. Ford trucks, usually with special bodywork, were operated by the military authorities of many countries. In the Soviet Union the Ford A, AA and a six-wheeled version of the AA were produced for many years, carrying the designations GAZ-A, GAZ-AA and GAZ-AAA respectively.

23A Ford

23B Ford

23C Ford

23A : **Ford** Model B four-cylinder pick-up truck, surviving in Great Britain. There was also a V8-engined model, distinguishable by V8 ornaments. Wheelbase was 106 in. Model B was produced during the 1932 model year and Model BB during 1932–34.

23B : **Ford** Model BB 1½-ton was also available with Four or V8 engine. Wheelbase was 131½ or 157 in. Shown is a 157-in V8 fire truck, equipped by A. Bikkers & Son of Rotterdam, Holland.

23C : **Ford** Model BB with right-hand drive and tandem rear axle bogie as produced in Great Britain. British Ford trucks were made and sold under the name Fordson.

24 : In 1933 **Ford** offered car-derived Model 46 ½-ton commercial
models and Model BB 1½-ton trucks, the latter with 131½- and 157-in
wheelbase. All were available with four- or eight-cylinder (V8) engine.
Shown is a military Model 46 112-in wb desert patrol vehicle, fitted
with oversize tyres, in the Middle East.

25B Ford

25A Ford

25C Ford/Thornton

25A : **Ford** Model BB trucks for 1934 were again available with 131½-
and 157-in wheelbase, and with 50-bhp four- or 80-bhp V-8-cylinder
engine. Shown is a long-wheelbase V8 with Dutch coachbuilt cab.
1934 styling of 1½-ton BB and ½-ton Model 46 was similar to 1933.
25B : **Ford** Model BB 1934 short-wheelbase tractor truck with standard
Ford Type 810 cab and fuel tanker semi-trailer.
25C : **Ford/Thornton** was a six-wheeler chassis with tandem-drive via
a central power divider which incorporated high and low gear ratios.
The axles were standard Ford, coupled directly to the power divider.

FWD, GARFORD, GMC

26A FWD

26B Garford

26A : **FWD** stood for four-wheel drive, but six-wheel drive variants also appeared as exemplified by this tractor unit with tandem axle semi-trailer for gasoline delivery. The unit could carry 5800 gallons of fuel, sufficient for the vehicle to run 25,000 miles if it were piped to its own carburettor!

26B : **Garford** trucks were, at this time, produced by Relay Motors Corp. and there were about eight basic models, from 1- to $5\frac{1}{2}$-ton capacity, all with Buda engines. This $2\frac{1}{2}$-ton 6 × 4 was a mobile mount for a 3·7-in anti-aircraft gun of the US Army, built in 1930/31.

26C : **GMC**, 'the Truck People of General Motors', in 1930 offered a very wide range of models, varying from $\frac{1}{2}$- to 15-ton payload rating. Most models were powered by engines from other GM divisions, namely Buick and Pontiac. The concrete mixer shown is on a Model T60 chassis, which had a 94-bhp Buick Six engine and 140-in wheelbase. T60 chassis prices ranged from $2800 to $3215. GMC also manufactured trailers.

26C GMC

27A GMC

27C GMC

27B GMC

27A: **GMC** Model T31 was available in four wheelbase lengths and had a 76-bhp six-cylinder Buick OHV engine with four-speed gearbox. Demonstrating the efficiency and practicality of the motor truck for the transport of perishable goods, in 1931 a GMC truck, with refrigerated trailer, delivered 21 tons of Californian fruit to New York in 117 hours' running time.
27B: **GMC** 1½-ton short-wheelbase model with 6·00-20 tyres and six-cylinder L-head Pontiac engine. 1932.
27C: **GMC** Series T30 tractor truck with bus semi-trailer. 1933 GMCs were similar to those of 1931/32 and there was a wide range of models to choose from.

28: **GMC** Model T61 tanker truck of the Texas Company. The heavy-duty T61 had a 5–6½-ton payload rating and was available with 145- or 154-in wheelbase. The engine was a 110-bhp OHV Six. 1934.

29C Gramm

29A GMC

29A: **GMC** of about 1934 still in service in Spain some 35 years later. The wide non-standard cab is of much later date than the truck.

29B: **Gotfredson** trucks were made in Canada (Walkerville, Ont.) as well as in Detroit, in the United States. This is a Canadian model of about 1931. Engines were the makers' own or Buda. The US operations of Gotfredson later became the Cummins Diesel Service and Sales of Michigan.

29C: **Gramm** trucks were made in Delphos, Ohio, from 1926 until the Second World War. This long-distance moving van of 1930 operated from Kansas City, Mo.

29B Gotfredson

INDIANA

30A Indiana

30A: In 1931 a Cummins four-cylinder Model U diesel engine was installed in an **Indiana** truck which was driven from New York to Los Angeles at an average speed of 43·02 mph. The 3214-mile journey took 97½ hours and the fuel cost was reported to be no more than $11.22.

30B: **Indiana** Motors Corp. of Marion, Indiana, had been owned by Brockway since 1928, but was purchased by White in 1932 and moved to Cleveland, Ohio, in the following year. Illustrated is a typical Indiana truck with dairy van body of 1932.

30C: **Indiana** heavy-duty chassis/cab for tractor or dump truck applications.

30B Indiana

30C Indiana

31A Indiana

31C Indiana

31B Indiana

31A: **Indiana** Model 85 1½-ton chassis with Hercules JXA six-cylinder 228 CID petrol engine cost $975 in 1933.

31B: **Indiana** Model 95 2-ton van-bodied truck in Boston, Mass. This model had a 282 CID Hercules JXC engine. 1933.

31C: **Indiana** truck chassis, as made by White, were in 1934 available in the Netherlands with Gardner-Kromhout four-cylinder diesel engine. This power unit replaced the original Hercules Six.

INTERNATIONAL

32A : **International** Model S24 was a popular 1¼-ton truck with four-cylinder Lycoming engine, Eaton axles and 130-in wheelbase. This specimen was assembled in England and fitted with hydraulic tipping gear.

32B : **International** Model 63 was a heavy-duty truck and a carryover from the late 1920s. Note the mounting of the headlamps on the sides of the cowl, a position where they were least vulnerable. Cab and body shown were made in England, *c.* 1930.

32C : **International** Harvester Co. of Great Britain offered this Hall Scott-engined Model W3 8-tonner as their heaviest truck in 1931.

32B International

32A International

32C International

33A International

33C International

34 : **International** tractor truck with semi-trailer in the logging industry. The A-line, of which this is another example, was superseded for 1935 by the entirely new and slightly-streamlined C-line.

33B International

33D International

33A : **International** Model A2 1½-ton chassis had a four-cylinder Waukesha engine. This furniture van was operated in Jersey, one of the British Channel Islands. 1933.
33B : **International** Model AL3 was offered in Britain in 1931 as a 2½–3-ton chassis with closed cab and various types of bodywork.
33C : **International** Harvester Co. produced light, medium and heavy trucks. Many were assembled overseas, including Britain where this

Model A5 4-tonner with RHD was supplied in 1932 to a firm of timber merchants.
33D : **International** A-line trucks ranged up to the 7½-ton Model A8. From Model A4 upwards they had the makers' own six-cylinder engines. This is one of the heavier models, operated by the Sinclair Petroleum Company in The Hague, Netherlands.

KENWORTH, LINN, MACK

36A Linn

37: **Mack** Model AC was a heavy-duty chain-drive chassis, production of which had started during the First World War. They were affectionately known as the 'Bulldog' and were later available with pneumatic tyres and as six-wheelers. The engine was a 75-bhp 5 × 6-in four-cylinder (AC4) or 125-bhp 4½ × 5½-in six-cylinder (AC6), both of Mack manufacture. Shown is an early Bulldog with tank body and tank trailer operated by Standard Oil (Esso).

36A: **Linn** Mfg. Corp. of Morris, NY, produced half-track tractors and trucks, mainly with dump, ballast and logging bodies. Hercules and Waukesha engines were used, and later a Cummins diesel was offered. A number of Linns were supplied to the US Army, from 1933. Shown is a 5-ton T6 (military designation) with 174-bhp Hercules HXE engine. Note horizontal position of steering-wheel. 1934.

36B: **Mack** Model BB was produced during the years 1928–32. An early model is shown. It was a 1½-ton truck with Mack AB four-cylinder engine. Transmission and axles were also made by Mack themselves. It was the lightest in the makers' extensive range which ran from 1½- to 15-ton models. In 1930 the BB chassis was listed at $3500.

35: **Kenworth** trucks were made in Seattle, Washington, from 1923. This photo of a typical semi-trailer rig was dated 1934. The company at this time used Buda, Hall Scott and Hercules six-cylinder engines, Timken transmissions, and other well-proven bought-in units. Models ranged from 1½–2-ton 87 to 5–7-ton 241C.

36B Mack

38: Another example of the famed **Mack** Bulldog. The exact date of manufacture of this unit is uncertain but production continued with detail modifications, until 1938 (see also Fig. 37). Tractor is shown hauling Marion shovel weighing 95,500 lb on Rogers 28-ton low-bed semi-trailer. Note the hinged funnel of the steam-powered shovel swung down in travelling position.

39C Mack

39A Mack

39B Mack

39A: In 1933 a **Mack** AB bus was fitted with a Cummins diesel engine for a coast-to-coast demonstration tour. The AB range was produced from 1914 until 1936, with periodic modifications and improvements.
39B: **Mack**, in addition to their well-known heavy-duty models, offered medium-sized trucks such as this model for payloads of about two tons. It had a six-cylinder engine and was supplied in 1932.
39C: **Mack** 'Bulldog' trucks had greatly helped in establishing the Mack name throughout the world. In 1933 the company announced: 'emblematic of their Bulldog breed is the miniature Bulldog figure that now adorns the radiator caps of all Mack trucks—whether with Bulldog or conventional hood or of hoodless Traffic Type design'.

MACK

40A Mack

40B Mack

40C Mack

40A: **Mack** Model BF 2½–4-ton trucks were produced from 1931 until 1939. They had a Mack six-cylinder engine of 90 bhp (governed to 79 bhp at 2300 rpm), Mack four-speed transmission (five-speed optional) and Mack dual-reduction rear axle.

40B: **Mack** Model BF of 1934 with special bodywork for refrigerated delivery work.
40C: **Mack** Model BQ was rated at 6–8-ton and is shown here with gasoline tank bodywork for Gulf, built in 1934. BQ production period: 1932–37.

41A Mack

41A : **Mack** Traffic Type forward control truck of 1933. At this time the cab-over-engine configuration was becoming popular again. The Traffic Type chassis was available in two versions : Model CH 3-5-ton and Model CJ 3½-6-ton, each with 150- or 186-in wheelbase. The CH had the Mack CE six-cylinder engine of 414 cu. in displacement (bore and stroke 4 × 5½ in), Mack BC double-reduction rear axle and 9.00-20 tyres. The heavier Model CJ had the Mack CF 468 CID Six engine with ¼-in larger bore, Mack BX double-reduction axle and 9.75-22 tyres. Both had the Mack BX four-speed transmission. Chassis prices with the standard 150-in wheelbase were, in 1934, $5200 and $6100 respectively.

41B : **Mack** Model BX tractor truck of 1934 with Fruehauf 12-ton van semi-trailer. In Britain such a rig would be called an 'articulated six-wheeler' or 'artic'. Mack BX trucks were in production during 1932—40. In 1934 the BX 3½-6-ton chassis was available with double-reduction rear axle or chain drive, the prices being $5600 and $5750 respectively (for standard wheelbase size). Both versions had the Mack Model CF 468 CID (4¼ × 5½ in) six-cylinder engine, driving through a Mack Model BX four-speed transmission. Tyre size was 9.75-22. The chain-drive model was 150 pounds heavier than the one with the live rear axle.

41B Mack

MARMON-HERRINGTON

42A Marmon-Herrington

Founders of the Marmon-Herrington Company, which was situated in Indianapolis, Indiana, were Walter C. Marmon and Colonel Arthur W. Herrington. The latter had been a Captain of the AEF in France during the First World War and during the 1920s, as an automotive engineer, had been involved in various all-wheel drive truck designs of the US Army's Quartermaster Corps, gaining wide experience and an enviable reputation in this field. Walter C. Marmon, also a distinguished automotive executive, had been the head of the famous motor-car manufacturing business, bearing his family name. Together they established a company which for several decades was one of the world's leading producers of all-wheel drive trucks, tractors, etc. From 1935 most of these vehicles were conversions of standard commercial Ford trucks.

42A –C: **Marmon-Herrington** was founded in 1931, and in 1932 built the first six-wheel drive tractor trucks for use by the IPC on the Iraq pipeline project across the Syrian desert. More were supplied in later years.

42B Marmon-Herrington

42C. Marmon-Herrington

43A Marmon-Herrington

43A: **Marmon-Herrington** of Indianapolis specialized in all-wheel drive and heavy-duty trucks. This was the first of the famous desert coaches for the Nairn Brothers' passenger and freight bus line between Damascus and Baghdad. The vehicle was 66 feet long and had luxury accommodation for 36 people. The tractor, a Model THD315 –6, powered by a Hercules diesel engine, was produced in 1932/33.

43B: **Marmon-Herrington** four-wheel-drive heavy-duty trucks were supplied for civilian and military use. Shown are some heavy dump trucks employed in road construction. They were powered by Hercules six-cylinder gasoline/petrol engines.

43B Marmon-Herrington

44 : **Oshkosh** built four-wheel-drive special
purpose trucks such as this 8-ton Model FDL.
It was powered by a Hercules RXLD 558 CID
gasoline engine, driving through a five-speed
Fuller gearbox and a two-speed Oshkosh
chain-drive transfer case incorporating an
automatic locking centre differential. The
vehicle was supplied in 1933 to the town of
Trenton in New York State.

45 : **Oshkosh** Model WLD 3 —3½-ton four-
wheel-drive truck of 1934 with dump body. It
had a 383 CID 106-bhp Hercules WXC3
six-cylinder engine. Tyres were 9·00-20
Balloon type, dual rear. The transmission was
either a Fuller 5-A-38 with five forward and
two reverse speeds or, at extra cost, a Fuller
5-A-380 with two-speed auxiliary gears
providing ten forward and two reverse speeds.
Transfer case was Oshkosh H1 single-speed.
Standard wheelbase was 146 in, but 165 and
201 in were also available.

PIERCE-ARROW

46A Pierce-Arrow

46A: **Pierce-Arrow** 5-ton stake truck of 1931/32 retained its classic radiator styling of the Teens and Twenties, but featured giant balloon tyres.
46B: **Pierce-Arrow** Model S50 2½–3-ton chassis with French Pillot 2½-cu. metre tipper body. Basically this was a Studebaker. Studebaker had acquired control of Pierce-Arrow in 1928 and sold trucks under this name until 1934.
46C: **Pierce-Arrow** period advertisement in Great Britain.

46B Pierce-Arrow

46C Pierce-Arrow

47B Relay

47A Relay

47A –C : **Relay** Motors Corporation of Lima, Ohio, offered this Model 300A dual-drive (6 × 4) six-wheeler, which was unusual in having twin Lycoming Model AEC eight-in-line 135-bhp engines, mounted side by side, and each driving one rear axle through two air-controlled 5F2R Fuller gearboxes. Other advanced features included Vickers hydraulic power steering, hydraulic clutch control, Westinghouse air brakes on all wheels and Cleco Gruss air springs at front. The cab embodied a single sleeping berth. Relay also made conventional trucks, with Buda six-cylinder engines.

47C Relay

48: **Reo** of Lansing, Michigan, were well known for their popular range of Speed Wagons, which were available with payload ratings from 1- to 3-ton. Shown is a Model F 1½-ton chassis with Reo Gold Crown six-cylinder (3⅜ × 5 in) L-head engine, four-speed transmission and spiral bevel rear axle. The bodywork was made and fitted in England.

49A Reo

49B Reo

49A: This 1931 **Reo** Speed Wagon has survived in Great Britain where, during the 1930s, the make was quite popular, particularly for bus and coach applications.
49B: Australia was another territory where the **Reo** was marketed. This advertisement of about 1933 emphasizes the Reo's ability to haul 'big sticks' in the timber country.
49C: **Reo** Speed Wagon heavy-duty chassis/cab with stake and platform body. 1932.

49C Reo

D

50 : **Reo** Speed Wagon range comprised many models, differing in engine, wheelbase, payload rating, etc. This beautifully restored furniture removal van of 1933 has been preserved in New Jersey.

51B Rockne

51A Reo

51C Rugby

51A : **Reo** 1934 Speed Wagon chassis with Gold Crown Six 7-bearing crankshaft engine. The coach body was fitted in Australia.
51B : **Rockne** Delivery Car of 1932. This panel van was derived from the Rockne Six passenger car which was produced by the Studebaker Corporation and named after football coach Knute Rockne.
51C : **Rugby** Model 6-15 DeLuxe Panel van as manufactured in 1932 by Dominion Motors Ltd of Leaside, Toronto, Canada. The body measured 102 × 58 × 48 in.

DURABILITY — ECONOMY — POWER — SPEED

52A : **Rugby** trucks were made by Durant Motors, Inc., of Lansing, Michigan, from 1928. There were four- and six-cylinder Continental-engined models from $\frac{1}{2}$- to $1\frac{1}{2}$-ton capacity. Thoroughly conventional in design, a fair proportion was exported. In 1932, however, production came to an end. Rugby trucks were also made in Canada (*see* 51C). This advertisement appeared in the summer of 1930.

52B : **Schacht** trucks were made from 1910 until 1938 in Cincinnati, Ohio. From 1927 until the end, the company name was The LeBlond-Schacht Truck Company. The 1930 programme comprised $1\frac{1}{2}$- to $7\frac{1}{2}$-ton four-wheelers, using Continental, Hercules and Waukesha engines. Transmissions, axles and most other components were also bought in from specialist manufacturers such as Brown-Lipe, Timken, Wisconsin, etc. Chassis prices ranged from $1765 up to $5200. The advertisement dates from late 1930.

RUGBY TRUCKS are Engineered *by* Experts to Cut Haulage Costs

The new and finer Rugby Trucks, built by Durant, are products of recognized experts who have studied every business in which transportation is a factor. They are engineered to cut haulage costs to the minimum.

Integral with the 6-cylinder engine is a specially designed *truck* transmis-sion, with direct drive in high and exceptionally low first-speed gear ratio.

This typifies the mechanical and structural features that distinguish the new Rugby — features vital to dependability and long life, and unobtainable at less than Rugby prices.

DURANT MOTORS, INC., EXPORT DIVISION
5057 WOODWARD AVE., DETROIT, U. S. A.
Factories: LANSING, MICH., OAKLAND, CAL., LEASIDE TORONTO, ONT.

RUGBY

A GOOD TRUCK - BUILT BY DURANT

52A Rugby

New SCHACHT DeLuxe Trucks Give Extra Performance — Extra Value

Every quality feature the seller or the buyer looks for is found in the New SCHACHT DeLuxe Models. The product of a manufacturer of over 20 years of experience in building good trucks, they are outstanding in performance, in appearance, in price, in value, in completeness of equipment. A size to meet every owner's requirements—1¼ to 7½ tons.

Write or Wire for Details.

THE LeBLOND-SCHACHT TRUCK CO.
Successful Motor Truck Manufacturers for Over 20 Years.
Factories in Cincinnati, Ohio, U. S. A.
Export Dept.: 44 Whitehall St., New York City, U. S. A.

52B Schacht

53A Sterling

53B Sterling

53C Sterling

53A : **Sterling** in 1930 produced four-wheeled trucks from $1\frac{1}{4}$- up to $5\frac{1}{2}$-ton capacity. Shown is an example of the $1\frac{1}{2}$-ton Model DB9-64-16C, which had 139-in wheelbase, 34 × 7 tyres and a Continental 16C six-cylinder engine. Like so many American trucks it featured Timken axles, Ross steering, and other well-proven components.
53B : **Sterling** Model FD80 3—4-tonner with six-cylinder (4 × $4\frac{3}{4}$ in) Waukesha 6ML engine, produced in 1931.
53C : **Sterling** heavy-duty six-wheeled truck chassis of about 1930. Note radiator guard, rear axle torque rods and absence of front wheel brakes. Sterling trucks were built in Milwaukee, Wisconsin.

STEWART

54A Stewart

55 : **Stewart** Model 42X 1¾-ton panel van of 1933. Like the Model 41X this truck had a 224 CID six-cylinder Lycoming engine. Wheelbase was 145 or 176 in.

54B Stewart

54C Stewart

54A : **Stewart** Motor Corporation of Buffalo, New York, in 1930/31 offered a wide range of models. Except for the heaviest models they used Lycoming four- and six-cylinder engines. All had Fuller clutches and transmissions. Rear axles were supplied by Clark and Timken. Chassis prices ranged from $695 for the Model 30 1-tonner up to $4990 for the heavy-duty Model 31X.

54B : **Stewart** Model 27X 5 –7-tonner with 4-cu. yd dump body. This truck had a Waukesha engine and Timken worm-drive rear axle. 1930/31.

54C : **Stewart** Model 41X ¾-ton panel van with six-cylinder Lycoming engine and 124-in wheelbase. 1933.

STEWART, STUDEBAKER

56A: **Stewart** chassis in 1934 were available with Lycoming six- and eight-cylinder engines. Some of the heavier types had a six-cylinder Waukesha. Illustrated is a bus chassis with streamlined coach bodywork, produced in the Netherlands.

56B: **Studebaker** in 1930 offered truck chassis from $845 up to $3695 with payload capacities from $\frac{3}{4}$ to $3\frac{1}{2}$ ton. They used their own engines and, on the lighter models, their own axles. Shown is a Model GK-N 146-in wheelbase 1-ton chassis with Dutch ambulance bodywork, operated in Amsterdam. This model had much in common with contemporary Studebaker cars and had a six-cylinder engine.

56C: **Studebaker** Model GN-N $1\frac{1}{4}$-ton truck with semi-trailer, also operated in the Netherlands. This model had the same engine as the GK-N, but used Clark transmission and rear axle with metal spoke wheels.

56B Studebaker

56A Stewart

56C Studebaker

57A: **Studebaker** Model S30 1½-ton chassis with own six-cylinder engine and special bodywork for the Dutch Tourist Club ANWB in The Hague. 1931.
57B: **Studebaker** Model S60 2-tonner with Dutch bodywork, delivered to an Amsterdam wine merchant in 1931.
57C: **Studebaker** 1932 2½-ton tank truck, powered by a six-cylinder L-head engine of 75 bhp.
At this time there was a short-lived merger of Studebaker and Pierce-Arrow (*q.v*) with White, and this illustration (together with Figs. 46A, 51B and 59A) appeared in a combined sales brochure of these three makes.

57A Studebaker

57B Studebaker

57C Studebaker

WARD LAFRANCE, WHITE

58A Ward LaFrance

58A: **Ward LaFrance** of Elmira, NY, produced a range of Waukesha-engined trucks and were specialists in manufacturing complete fire trucks of which this preserved specimen, dating from 1933, is a fine example.

58B: **White** Model 60 of 1929/30 was a 1-ton chassis, priced at $1850. The cab was an extra-cost option. It had a White 2A six-cylinder engine. The same truck was available with four-cylinder engine at $1545 (Model 15B). Both had 30 × 5 tyres, single at rear.

58C: **White** heavy-duty tractor truck with semi-trailer for long-distance haulage. Note the air horns on the cab roof and the 'W' emblem on the front bumper. *c.* 1930

58B White

58C White

59A White

59C White

59A: **White** heavy six-wheeler with tandem axle drive of 1932.

59B: **White** heavy-duty long-wheelbase chassis with attractive furniture removal van bodywork in New York, *c.* 1931.

59C: **White** Model 58S 7½-ton tractor truck with four-wheel semi-trailer plus a similar trailer with dolly converter. Engine was a White GRB four-cylinder ($4\frac{1}{4} \times 5\frac{3}{4}$ in). 1931/32.

59D: **White** tractor truck with Dutch cab and Werkspoor semi-trailer, specially designed for transporting heavy rolls of newsprint paper in the Netherlands.

59B White

59D White

60: **White** Model 691 tractor truck with two semi-trailers, the second operating as a full-trailer by means of a dolly converter. 1932.

61C White

61A White

61B White

61A: **White** in 1933 offered over 30 standard truck chassis, including this Model 612 2½–3-tonner. Unlike most other American truck makers, White manufactured their own engines, transmissions, axles and other components.
61B: **White** Model 701 1¼-ton chassis with panel delivery body. It had a 240 CID White 8A Six engine. 1934.
61C: **White** chassis/cowl, fitted with Kromhout-Gardner diesel engine which was optional at extra cost in the Netherlands.

... in Heavy Hauling

THESE BUSINESSES NEED UNDERSLUNG POWER TRANSPORTATION

City and Intercity Haulers
Contract Haulers
Oil Companies
Bulk Milk Haulers
Dairies
Chain Stores
Coal Dealers
Furniture Stores
Moving and Storage Companies
Dump Truck Operators
Manufacturers who truck their goods to market

STAR TRANSFER COMPANY

This diagrammatic view of the new *Underslung Power* White shows the location of the engine and the principal mechanical units. The Pancake design of the engine permits a cab with a perfectly flat floor of conventional overall height, thus eliminating two chief disadvantages of cab-over-engine trucks using conventional power plants.

NEW

"Underslung Power!"

62 : **White** introduced their 'Underslung Power' truck in 1934. It was powered by a horizontally-opposed L-head 12-cylinder 'Pancake' engine. Shown is the Model 731T 100-in wheelbase tractor version.

63A White

63B Willys

63A : **White** in 1934 offered chassis with payload ratings ranging from 1¼ to 9 tons. These are sightseeing coaches (Bear Mountain Park) on one of the lighter chassis.

63B : **Willys** 1½-ton stake truck of 1932. Willys-Overland had commenced truck production in 1930 at their Toledo, Ohio, plant.

63C : End of the road : a group of discontinued Mobil tank trucks at the company's Waltham, Massachusetts, terminal in 1942. Most of the vehicles date from the early 1930s. The truck in the centre foreground is a GMC.

63C Mobil tank trucks

INDEX

ABBREVIATIONS

bhp	brake horsepower
CID	cubic inches displacement
L-head	side-valve (engine)
OHV	overhead valves
q.v.	quod vide (which see)
rpm	revolutions per minute
wb	wheelbase

ACKNOWLEDGEMENTS

This book was compiled and written largely from historic source material in the library of the Olyslager Organisation, and in addition photographs and/or other material was kindly provided or loaned by Messrs. Larry Auten, Jan Bakker, Sven Bengtson, John Carter, Arthur J. Ingram, G. A. Ingram, Jean-Gabriel Jeudy, Fred C. Lane, John B. Montville, William F. Murray, Jan Polman, Stanley C. Poole, Ken Taylor, and R. A. Wawrzyniak, as well as several manufacturers and organisations, notably : Automobile Manufacturers Association, Inc., Brockway Motor Trucks, Chrysler Corp., General Motors Corp., International Harvester (Great Britain) Ltd., Mack Trucks, Inc., Mobil Oil Corp., OLD MOTOR, Oshkosh International, Inc., Texaco Ltd., and White Motor Corp.

-0. DEC. 1979